MIKE GOLDSWORTHY

IN GOD
WE TRUST?

WHEN THE KINGDOM OF GOD
AND POLITICS COLLIDE

In God We Trust?
When the Kingdom of God and Politics Collide

Edited and compiled by Ashley Wolpert Miller
Additional editing by Marcia Graham
Cover Design by Brent Otey

Live Contrarian
Long Beach, CA 90808

ISBN: 978-0692645864

To the Parkcrest Elders

Thank you for always encouraging me to pursue my convictions

CONTENTS

INTRODUCTION

There are two things your mom always told you not to talk about at parties if you want to be polite: religion and politics.

These topics are so personal and emotionally charged that their appearance drives light-hearted conversation into arguments and fighting the world over.

So, when I decided to write a book, I thought— why not write about religion *and* politics? That should go over well and not stir up any controversy.

Here's the deal: I will probably end up offending you at some point as you read through the following pages. If you're a Republican, I'm going to offend you. Don't worry: If you're a Democrat, I'm going to offend you, too. If you're a Libertarian, a member of the Tea Party, a registered independent—you can count on being offended as well. Much of the content here I derived from a sermon series I taught in 2012. During that series, somebody told me, "you didn't talk enough about the Whig party." If you somehow consider yourself a part of the Whig party, I'll do my best to offend you as well.

In writing, I have made a few assumptions that are foundational to my arguments. I believe it's important first to acknowledge these assumptions.

Assumption One
The Scriptures are authoritative.

Maybe you've picked up this book, and you don't believe that's true. That's okay, and there is space for you to investigate and figure all of that out. But for those of us who follow Jesus, we believe that God is our authority, and he has mediated that authority to us through Scripture.

The Scriptures are where God has mediated his authority—not The Constitution or the founding fathers. Political talking heads aren't our authority, nor the president, nor the candidate de jour; the Bible is. That's my starting point.

Assumption Two
Dialogue is helpful.

In our highly politicized and polarized environment, it is incredibly hard to have an actual conversation. An off-the-cuff statement swiftly turns into a 24-hour news cycle. We talk past one another. We just have talking points we say to each other. We want to tell the other person what we think, and that person doesn't want to dialogue; they just want to tell us what *they* think.

In October of 2012, *TIME* Magazine ran a cover story written by Michael Scherer[1], which referenced a couple of fascinating studies. In 2006, Brendan Nyhan, of Dartmouth, and research partner Jason Reifler, then of Georgia State University, found that if you take a group of people with a particular political leaning and show them facts that contradict that political posture, most people will not believe facts that collide with their bent.

Nyhan and Reifler discovered that this is true for people who lean politically right, and it is true for people who lean politically left. Neither side is more open to facts. Both of them are averse to information that pushes against their preconceived political narratives.

In fact, Scherer's article referenced a second 2006 study by a researcher, and then Princeton graduate student, named Danielle Shani that I found even more fascinating. It further showed that the more politically engaged and informed a person is, the less likely they are to be open to facts.

Some of you have friends you're thinking of right now. Some of you *are* that friend.

The more we care about politics, and the more this political bent becomes integrated into our worldview, the more difficult it becomes to admit when we're wrong, or when the group we affiliate with is wrong. According to Scherer,

> "... more factual information might seem like a good solution to [the] problem [of bias]. But the reality is more complex. Researchers have demonstrated ... that pieces of false information, once heard, establish themselves as 'belief echoes' that can persist even after a falsehood is corrected."

The more informed you are, the less inclined you are to *believe* facts that conflict with your opinions. The more informed you are, the less inclined you are to *respond* to facts that conflict with your views. Scherer writes that in Shani's study, "those with more information exhibited a bias 5.5 times larger than those who knew less."

Five and a half times.

So what is all this saying? It's saying that we don't want dialogue. We might say we want dialogue, but what we want is to be affirmed in what we already believe—affirmed in the direction we're already moving. Who won the last debate? Well, it depends on what narrative you ascribed to at the time you sat down to watch.

You work to find people that support your argument. You search to find opinion pieces that support it. You dig to find a quote from an individual that supports your narrative.

But what if there is a different way? What if we still can have actual dialogue? What if we can learn to listen to one another?

As Christians, we are supposed to be people who seek truth. Jesus said at one point,

> "I am the way and the truth and the life" (John 14:6).

A part of seeking Jesus is seeking truth. We're not people who seek a particular political ideology or a specific political narrative. We're people who seek truth. So what if by being a people who seek truth first and foremost—above our political narratives—we could have conversation. I want to suggest that we can be people who come to some different conclusions, but because we're seekers of truth, we're people able to dialogue.

Assumption Three
This book begins discussion.

My intention is to spur on conversations that ignite other conversations. This book is intended to get us talking. What I write here I do not mean to be the conclusive, final word. Wrap a bow on it. We're done. This is what the church believes, and everyone who's a part of the church has to accept these things.

This text is not intended to be that.

My hope is that you'll read this book in the way that I ask my church to hear my sermons. That this begins the conversation rather than ends it.

Some of you are incredibly politically engaged. You have strong opinions, and you're thinking, *I am not going to let someone tell me what to think or how to vote. He doesn't understand what he's writing. He hasn't been around as much. He hasn't seen what I've seen.*

I've been told these things as I've engaged in these conversations. What I've learned is that for some of you, you have your narrative, and it doesn't matter what I say or really what anyone else says. You're not going to change anything.

There are members of my church who serve as elected officials or who work for those in office. There are others who work as lobbyists. If you're in one of those camps, you are already engaged in a political narrative for the most part—and you likely have strong opinions.

Some of you moderately engage in politics. You keep up with it. You watch the debates or, at least, portions of them. You read political news stories, but you don't make your opinions known. You're not posting stuff on social media. You're not putting signs in your yard. You just keep it to yourself, but you're pretty informed and interested in what's going on.

Then the rest of you have turned off social media during election seasons, and you've stopped watching the news. You're in this place where you think, *I just don't want to talk to people right now, because it gets so politically charged and so, "he said, she said." I just don't wish to deal with that.* You just want to ignore it all. Your hope is that it will all go away quickly so that everyone can get back to normal.

Regardless of which of those describes you, here's what I want you to know: My goal is not to get you to vote a certain way, and my goal is not to say that what I write here is the definitive answer. My goal is to get you to have conversations that maybe you are not currently having. It's to cause you to ask questions that maybe you're not currently asking. If all I do is encourage conversation, to me—that's a win.

CHAPTER 1. What We Want to Hear

The temptation for a pastor is to say or do things that won't ruffle feathers in their church. Just a few months before the 2008 U.S. presidential election, I was hired as the lead pastor at Parkcrest Christian Church in Long Beach, California. I made a decision during that election season, one based on a long precedent in our church, that we weren't going to engage from the stage in any political commentary.

Some members of our church were pretty bothered by that. We had some good discussions and email exchanges as we talked about why as a church we had chosen to do that. I still think that was the right decision for us to have made at that time, but I also realize now that a part of the reason people were so upset then was that we hadn't helped them to frame the political conversation yet. There were plenty of others who were helping them frame it, but we hadn't contributed.

We didn't do that for a few reasons. First, I couldn't have articulated it well then. I couldn't have said what I wanted to say at that point. After spending the last several years thinking about this and praying about it and studying, I can be much more articulate today in expressing what I want to say than I could have years ago. I can be much more articulate about what I understand the Scriptures to be saying in this regard. Undoubtedly I will learn and grow in my ideas and attitudes in the future as well. However, I am confident and convicted that it is time to speak out with what I understand today to be true and clear—in order to spur on the conversation.

The second reason is this: I'll just confess I was scared to talk about it because people can get mean about this. I've found in the church that if you talk about something that people are passionate and opinionated about, and you don't merely affirm what they already believe, they tend to get pretty upset. In fact, there's this warning the apostle Paul gives his young apprentice Timothy that has stuck with me. In 2 Timothy 4 he says,

> "[People] will gather around them a great number of teachers to say what their itching ears want to hear."

He's saying what's going to happen is people are going to find teachers who are just going to say what they want them to say. Teachers who will affirm what they already believe.

Sometimes you'll hear people talk about this passage, and they'll say things like, *this is what pastors are doing today. They're trying to reach people outside the church, and so they're just watering down the gospel to tell them what they want to hear.* That's not at all what Paul is referencing.

He's not talking about people outside the church. Paul is addressing those inside the church. He's saying that what's going to happen is people in the church are going to start to listen to teachers who say what they want them to say, who affirm what they already believe.

The temptation is to search for a pastor or teacher, to *want* a pastor or teacher, to confirm merely what you already think and believe and how you already live. The temptation for me, as a pastor and author, is to do simply that for you and to placate Christians.

I write all of that to let you know up front that I have moved past being scared and moved beyond my concern with how people will react to what I have to say, because the Scriptures have convicted me.

One day I will have to stand before the Lord. One day I have to stand before God and give an account for what I did through my teachings. I will have to account for how I spoke and how I wrote, and I want to stand before God one day judged on how I preached my convictions from the Scriptures rather than how I said what I thought the people in the church wanted to hear.

So here's what I want to ask you to do as you read: If you would, just listen and don't reject what I write about because it pushes against things you already think or believe. Ask questions like: *Is this biblical? Does this stand up to the character of Jesus?* Those are the kinds of questions we should be asking as the church.

CHAPTER 2. The Means Matter

When we talk about politics, what we need to
understand is that everything political is about
how we accomplish all that we need and want to
achieve as a society. As an individual, you have a
certain end and a certain goal or goals you are
after. For many of you, the way you engage in
politics is centered on a particular social effect
you're after. Some of you are passionate about
ending abortion, and some of you are passionate
about caring for illegal immigrants, and some of
you are passionate about the government
defining marriage in a certain way, and some of
you are passionate about unjust working
conditions or a living wage or maybe religious
liberties and freedoms.

Regardless of the end results we are passionate
about, what we're doing when we engage in the
political process is using political means to try
and achieve those specific ends. The way the
political process works is that you gain power,
control, and influence to attempt to enact laws
that will then require people to live a certain
way that you believe is best.

In the 1980's, a group of evangelical Christians
recognized the U.S. political system as one that

they could use to achieve a social end they believed to be best. They founded the Moral Majority, which essentially said, *if we can get evangelical Christians recognized as a significant voting bloc, we will hold a lot of power and sway in America. We can get things in this country to happen the way that we want them to.* The Moral Majority gained traction and utilized politics as means to gain power and control to advance what they understood a kingdom lifestyle to look like.[1]

For many Christians, this became a normative expectation—that our goal is to utilize the political process to gain power to bring about transformation in our society.

It probably won't surprise you to learn that Jesus had a thing or two to say about power and control and how his followers use it. There's an account of a time when Jesus' disciples are on the road, and one of their mothers begins to lobby for influence and power for her sons. In response,

> "Jesus called [his disciples] together and said, 'You know that the rulers of the Gentiles lord it over them, and their high officials exercise authority over them'" (Matthew 20:25).

He says that there's a group of people—they're associated with the Gentiles—and here's what they do: Their rulers and high officials lord it over the people. In other words, they get into positions of power and authority, and they use that power and authority to manipulate, to coerce and to control people toward their desired end. Just to reiterate his point, he says,

> "… their high officials exercise authority over them."

They use being in positions of power over others to get people to do what they want them to do. Notice Jesus is not saying anything about the end they're going after. He's not saying anything about the goals they're trying to achieve. For all we know, they could be going after great goals. They could have the same goals for society and others that you do. That's not what he's talking about here. What he is concerned with is the way in which they achieve those goals.

What Jesus describes is what Greg Boyd refers to as a "power over" structure of influence. In a "power over" structure, one group (or one person) exercises authority over others to get them to do something.

Boyd talks about it this way in his book, *Myth of a Christian Nation*[2]:

> "While it comes in many forms, the kingdom of the world is in essence a 'power over' kingdom. In some versions —such as America—subjects have a say in who their rulers will be, while in others they have none. In some versions, subjects may influence how their rulers exercise power over them—for example, what laws they will live by—while in others they do not. There have been democratic, socialist, communist, fascist, and totalitarian versions of the kingdom of the world, but they all share this distinctive characteristic: they exercise 'power over' people."

In this kind of structure, one influences how others think and feel by attempting to control behavior. Behavior is controlled in a few ways.

Behavior is controlled through punishment and laws. Take a practical example from my life. When I leave my neighborhood, there is a No Left Turn street sign. The problem is that the freeway is to my left, and it's convenient to make a left-hand turn. One day, I was running late and didn't want to hassle going the long way, so I made a left-hand turn. When I saw blue and red lights in my rearview mirror, I experienced "power over," firsthand. I have never again made a left turn as I leave my neighborhood. Someone in a position of authority determined that they didn't want people to make left turns at this intersection, and utilizing tickets as punishment they changed my behavior.

Behavior is also controlled through things like wars and killing. If I want to change the decisions that you're making, I can threaten you or drop bombs on you to try and force you—out of fear and under threat—to make different decisions. Whether it's through utilizing punishment or wars, it's all about gaining and using power over people to control their behavior.

The goal in this kind of system is to change people's external behavior.

Jesus says this is what the Gentiles do.

For Jewish persons in the first century, Gentile was a shorthand way of saying those who are outside of the community of God, or those who don't subscribe to the ways of God. Essentially, it's another way of calling them pagans. Jesus describes what they do: They get into positions of power and authority so that they can have power over others to control their behavior. They may be doing it to achieve good results, or perhaps to achieve evil end results—we don't know. We know that they work to gain power over them.

Jesus then says,

> "Not so with you. Instead, whoever wants to become great among you must be your servant, and whoever wants to be first must be your slave—just as the Son of Man did not come to be served, but to serve, and to give his life as a ransom for many"
> (Matthew 20:26-28).

He's essentially telling those that have signed up to be his disciples that in his community, the rules are different.

Jesus sets up a contrast. He's saying there is the way of the Gentiles, and then there's this other way for those who are his followers. Remember,

Jesus is not describing the end they're trying to achieve. He is talking specifically about the way in which that end is achieved. He says, *with me, it is all about service and sacrifice and giving up your life.*

He is saying that his way of influence, the way things are achieved in his kingdom, the way you get to a certain end, is not by gaining power and using that power to control the behavior of the people. In Jesus' kingdom, it's entirely different. *His kingdom* is about serving and sacrifice and giving up your life.

You may be going after the right result, but there's a way of getting there that is the antithesis of Jesus. There's also a way of accomplishing your goal that aligns with the ways of Jesus.

The way of the world, the way of the Gentiles, is "power over." It's about getting into positions of authority to gain power over people, so you can exercise that authority and power to get people to do what you think is best for them to do. On the other hand, there is the way of Jesus and his kingdom. It is a way that influences people through service and sacrifice and death. To Jesus, the means matter very much. The way in which you achieve your goal, the way you go after your end—it matters.

Far too often, when we talk about politics and the church, politics and Jesus, or politics and the kingdom, our conversation is all about the end goal. It's all about the kinds of results we want to see. If you're on the religious right, your end goals are all about things like abortion and gay marriage, and if you are on the religious left, your end goals are all about things like workers' rights and immigration and the poor.

When it comes to politics, things are tremendously contentious among Christians. Could the reason be that we are having the wrong conversation? Could the reason there is so much fighting, even among Christians, be that we keep talking and arguing about end goals— all the while assuming that politics is the means by which we should be trying to achieve those goals? All the while missing that Jesus seems very, very concerned with the means—with the way in which we get there? To Jesus the ends matter, but the means by which we achieve those ends seems to matter at least as much.

We're being used by the political system, and we're the ones who lose in the end. What if the religious right has it wrong, and what if the religious left has it wrong? What if we are having the wrong conversation? Maybe we need to rethink the framework through which we are having this conversation.

Could it be that we're trying to utilize a political system to see the kingdom of God grow and spread while Jesus has a different intention for how it will grow? There are two predominant metaphors Jesus uses to describe the way his kingdom spreads. Matthew records him saying this:

> "He told them another parable: 'The kingdom of heaven is like a mustard seed, which a man took and planted in his field. Though it is the smallest of all seeds, yet when it grows, it is the largest of garden plants and becomes a tree, so that the birds come and perch in its branches.' He told them still another parable: 'The kingdom of heaven is like yeast that a woman took and mixed into about sixty pounds of flour until it worked all through the dough"
> (Matthew 13:31-33)

He uses these two pictures, two metaphors to describe the way the kingdom grows. The kingdom is like a mustard seed, the smallest of all seeds. It's something that's small, and it's planted. It takes root, and then it grows and grows and grows. Then he says it's also like yeast, something that's small and then as it gets mixed in it begins to work its way through the dough, affecting the whole thing.

The two predominant metaphors Jesus uses to describe the kingdom growing are about something small that grows and grows and something that gets mixed in and works its way through. You never find Jesus describing his kingdom as one which grows by the acquisition of power. The kingdom is never described as one that grows by getting people to act or forcing them to act like they are kingdom people. It is never described as a top-down movement. It's always described as something that builds and grows.

Jesus' concern is with changing people's hearts and minds in such a way that the result is changed behavior. That's why the kingdom spreads as yeast or a mustard seed—because it spreads one person at a time. It spreads through interior transformation. As Jesus changes who you are, you begin to act differently and respond differently, and you begin to care about different things. Your external behavior changes, but it changes as an overflow of interior transformation.

This stands in contrast to the way we often engage in politics, which is all about trying to get power over people to then enact laws that move people to change their external behavior.

Let me give an example that illustrates how we've done this in a way that we're a bit removed from so that perhaps we can be more objective about it.

Prohibition.

In the late nineteenth century and bleeding into the twentieth, many societal problems were being linked with increased alcohol consumption. Things like decreased worker productivity; increased poverty; drunk husbands who abused their wives and didn't provide stable homes and incomes; increased crime; increased political corruption—these issues were all linked with increased alcohol consumption.

A movement began, largely led by pastors and churches[3], called The Temperance Movement. By the late nineteenth century, members of the movement were seeking to abolish alcohol because of the abuse and the consequences of it. 1919 saw the ratification of the eighteenth amendment, which prohibited the production, the transportation and the sale of alcoholic beverages.[4, 5, 6]

The amendment went into effect in 1920 and historians say it would not have passed without the efforts of pastors—without the support of Christians and their churches. In some ways, you could say it worked. Alcohol consumption dropped by more than half per capita. Unfortunately, however, it had unintended consequences. Because of that law, crime and corruption rose significantly and created a culture in which the number of organized crime rings began to increase as well.

It began to be suggested that not only would prohibition fail, but it would ultimately end up undermining respect for all laws.[7] It was determined that prohibition didn't live up to its promise of making America safer, more productive, more moral, or more prosperous. In 1933, the amendment was repealed.[8]

Why didn't it work? Because you can't legislate morality. You can't legislate transformation.

We all know that alcohol abuse has significant ramifications. Some of us have had personal experience with alcohol that has significantly shaped our lives or the lives of people we care about. But the mistake early twentieth century Christians made was instead of helping individuals to know and understand the significance of Jesus, and walking with them through conquering their addictions, they decided instead that the best way to achieve kingdom results was to utilize the political process and to exert power over.

Today we don't even have that conversation, at least about prohibition. I have never had anyone in my church approach me and ask why we aren't lobbying to abolish alcohol. It's not even a conversation anymore. We know the best way to deal with it is at an individual level through programs like Celebrate Recovery[9], because that's how the kingdom grows. It grows like a mustard seed. It grows like yeast. Not through laws and not through constitutional amendments.

There are certain ways in which those of us who are followers of Jesus live—behaviors and ends we work toward or ways of living we ascribe to. What we are often doing is trying to use politics as a means to get others to live that way as well. When we do that, do we ever stop and consider the result of doing so? The result is that there are people who are living out the right exterior actions without any actual internal transformation.

The discussions Christians have around politics are too often centered on questions like: *How do we use the political process to best achieve our desired results? To best achieve the things that we want?* I wonder if we need to ask a question before that. Maybe first we should ask: *Is this the best system to try and achieve kingdom results?*

Let's go back to Jesus. Who was it that Jesus had the most conflict with during his lifetime? It was the religious leaders of his day, and most specifically the Pharisees and the teachers of the law. What was his biggest issue with them? Over and over again he would say things like, you have the right external behavior, you are following all of the laws, but your heart is far from me.

In one account recorded by Matthew, he's laying into the Pharisees pretty hard when he says to them:

> "Woe to you, teachers of the law and Pharisees, you hypocrites! You are like whitewashed tombs, which look beautiful on the outside but on the inside are full of the bones of the dead and everything unclean. In the same way, on the outside you appear to people as righteous but on the inside you are full of hypocrisy and wickedness"
> (Matthew 23:27-28)

He's saying, you are good at the outward things. You're good at following the law. You're doing all of the right external actions, but it doesn't matter if an internal change hasn't occurred. In fact, just before this in Matthew 23, as he's giving these "woes" to the Pharisees and teachers of the law, he essentially says: Here's how you change. You clean the inside first. You change the inside first. You have an interior transformation (Matthew 23:26).

He uses the metaphor of a cup, saying,

> "Blind Pharisee! First clean the inside of
> the cup and dish, and then the outside
> also will be clean"
> (Matthew 23:26)

What Jesus is saying is, you don't change your
behaviors and then expect that you'll have an
internal change. Instead, you are changed
internally and then that begins to overflow to
change the way you're living externally.

If that's the case, isn't it then that what we are
doing by trying to use political means to bring
about kingdom ends actually advocating for the
creation of a nation of Pharisees?

You may be thinking, *no, no, that's not what we're
doing. Here's what we're doing: There's a system
that's available to us; why shouldn't we use it? It just
makes practical sense. It's pragmatic. It is the most
expedient way to get it done. We should use all of the
means that are available to us to achieve kingdom
ends, because the other way you're talking about—
that's not efficient, that feels slow. It sounds nice—
Jesus talked about seeds and yeast—but this is the
real world. We don't have time for those stories. Here,
the rubber meets the road, and we actually have to
deal with this stuff. So we should use the systems of
the culture and the world to achieve our desired result*

because that is the most efficient and most practical way to get there.

Jesus over and over again seems very unconcerned with pragmatism, because to him the means matter. It's not just the results, but it's the way in which you get there. Jesus thought the means mattered not only for his disciples but him as well. He took that same criteria, and he lived by it.

In John 18, as Jesus is put on trial, false charges are being brought against him. He could have done something about all of that. He could have used the means through which everyone else accomplished their goals. He could have used the means of the world, and honestly, it would have been the most practical solution for him. However, look at what he says:

> "My kingdom is not of this world. If it were, my servants would fight to prevent my arrest by the Jewish leaders. But now my kingdom is from another place" (John 18:36)

He's saying, the systems by which my kingdom operates are completely different systems and structures than by which the kingdoms of the world operate. He's saying, I could give into the kingdom of the world to accomplish my end, but I will not, because my kingdom operates differently.

What he's communicating is this: The way everyone else would do it—the expedient way, even, of doing it—would be to have my followers rise against the leaders—to have them take up arms against those who have taken me. But my kingdom does not operate according to the normal way of doing things.

There have been movements throughout church history, and there are movements today where Christians intentionally choose to abstain from the political process—not because they're tired of empty rhetoric and not because they'd have to choose the best of two bad options, as you hear so many people say. Instead, they have intentionally abstained from the political process because they've said that to engage in it is to give into the systems and the structures of the world, that it's to operate by the rules of the world rather than by the rules of the kingdom.

I don't think that's where you have to end up as you read this book. Maybe some of you will end up in that place, but I don't think that's where you have to end up and that's not what I'm advocating, and it's not where I have ended up.

But I do want you to know that that these movements have existed and exist today, because the rhetoric you often hear in church circles is that you have a Christian responsibility and civic duty to vote, and I just want you to know that not everyone believes that. There are thoughtful and engaging men and women who are dedicated followers of Jesus, who throughout history would completely disagree with that statement.

John Roth, writing out of the Mennonite tradition in *Electing Not to Vote*, writes this as one of his arguments for choosing to abstain from voting,

> "… North American Mennonites could choose not to vote as a kind of 'spiritual discipline'—a tangible reminder that our ultimate identity is not contingent upon the political process or dependent on the powers that be. Combined with a clear commitment to care for the sick, to feed the hungry, and to bind up the wounds of the hurting, conscientious abstention from the presidential elections could be a

> powerful symbol of our conviction that true power—the primary locus of God's hand in history—resides ultimately in the gathered church, not among the policy makers in Washington D.C."[10]

They would say that your duty and your responsibility as a Christian is to abstain from the political process because in giving in to that process you are giving in to the kingdoms of the world. This is one way that some Christian traditions view the political process, and perhaps it's worth examining some of the assumptions you have made or heard about how Christians should engage in politics.

Jesus says the way his kingdom operates is not normal. In fact, often in a kingdom framework, the very things that make it look like you are losing to everyone else are the result of winning. The cross is a perfect example of this. When the apostle Paul talks about the cross in Colossians 2, specifically talking about Jesus, he says,

> "And having disarmed the powers and authorities, he made a public spectacle of them, triumphing over them by the cross" (Colossians 2:15)

The cross is a moment of triumph for Jesus. On the cross, he makes a public spectacle of the powers and authorities, but to most of the outside observers and to the powers and authorities, it looks like he has lost on the cross. His followers have deserted him. The Jewish officials claim victory and the Romans think they have killed him.

Sometimes when you step back to look at things through a kingdom framework, when it looks like you are winning according to the means and rules and ways of the world—sometimes you are losing.

Jesus chooses not to do the reasonable thing, the normal, expected thing—the thing that would make the most pragmatic, practical sense. Instead, he chooses the cross. The very symbol that for everyone else means loss, for him means triumph.

Do we trade in a kingdom framework to try and win on the world's terms?

I hardly ever find us asking if this political system is the right way to achieve kingdom results. I am entirely convinced that Jesus is not just concerned about the ends we achieve or the results we get, but he is entirely concerned as well with the means by which we get there, because to Jesus, the means matter.

To Jesus, the means matter.

That's why the kingdom is not ushered in by typical means—with power, coercion and force. That's why Jesus doesn't give in to the systems of the world to achieve his kingdom goals. That's why he instead goes to the cross to achieve those goals. That's why he goes to the symbol of shame and disrespect and dies the death of a common criminal—because to triumph in the kingdom looks different.

To triumph in the kingdom looks different.

Sometimes in the kingdom, when it looks to everyone else like you are losing, you're winning. Sometimes in the kingdom, when it looks to everyone else like you are winning, you are actually losing. In the long run, using politics to try and legislate morality doesn't work. It doesn't work because that's not how Jesus' kingdom spreads. Jesus isn't just concerned with the end; he's concerned with the means by which we get there.

The thing is, because we don't fully get that mindset, we often instead choose the most practical route, the route that leads to quick results, the route that's there in front of us. Part of the reason we do that, if we're to be honest, is out of fear. That's what happens during the election season.

Fear drives the way that we engage in elections.

CHAPTER 3. Fear and Politics

Most ads, whether about a proposition or a politician, are based on what happens if you elect this person or don't elect that person, or what happens if this proposition is or isn't passed. It's all about scaring us. They are fear-based ads about what could happen if you vote in one direction or another.

There's one well-known Christian organization that, in 2008, before Barack Obama was elected, wrote a letter from 2012 looking back over the last four years. It was supposed to be a letter from the future. It contained 34 predictions of what could be true in 2012 if Obama were to be elected president. If you were to read through this letter, what you'd find is that every single one of those predictions is rooted in fear. Not a single one of them is something positive that could happen or hopeful in any way. The predictions are 100 percent fear based.

In 2012, some people dug that letter back up. They looked over those predictions and went through every one of them to ask: Did these come to fruition at all? Here's what they found: Of the 34 predictions they laid out there, one of them partially happened but didn't fully happen, and the other 33 predictions didn't even come close to happening. The letter had nothing to do with the gospel of Jesus and living out the gospel of Jesus. It had nothing to do with pursuing truth or trying to accurately predict the trajectory of situations. It had everything to do with perpetuating a certain political agenda.

If you want to perpetuate a political agenda, you scare people into wanting to move in your direction. We already know this is what politicians do. If you've ever watched any of the U.S. presidential debates, if you've seen any of the ads, if you read any of the political blogs, if you listen to talk radio, if you keep up with cable news at all—they spend an inordinate amount of time trying to scare you. Here's what could happen if this person gets elected. Here's what could happen if this proposition passes or doesn't pass. That's what the political process does.

I remember reading David McCullough's excellent book on John Adams, and realizing that these same tactics were used when John Adams ran against Thomas Jefferson.[1,2] We should expect that's what the political process is because apparently that works, and apparently that's built into the system, and it's what's been done since the early days of the American political process. But I will just tell you this: Making decisions out of fear is a terrible way to live, and you are called to something better than that. In fact, here's how the apostle John puts it:

> "There is no fear in love. But perfect love drives out fear, because fear has to do with punishment. The one who fears is not made perfect in love"
> (1 John 4:18)

Pay attention to what he's saying here. He says perfect love—God's love that has been revealed in Jesus—If you've experienced that, it drives out fear. We are not a people who perpetuate fear, and we are not a people who are driven by, manipulated by or who make choices out of fear.

You may be reading this as someone who is passionate and politically zealous. You are concerned about certain causes and a particular person running for office—and the way in which you talk about it, the articles you're passing around, the emails you're forwarding, the things you're posting on social media, are all about perpetuating fear. If that's you, take a moment and pull up your Facebook feed and read the last few political posts that you posted. Or turn on your favorite cable news station and pay attention to the stories they tell and the way that they tell them. Does the narrative have an undercurrent of fear?

A basic posture for those of us who follow Jesus is that we are not people who perpetuate fear. You may have a great end in mind, but to Jesus, *the means matter*. The way in which you try and achieve that end matters—and perfect love drives out fear.

You may remember a highly publicized proposition in California during the 2008 election, Proposition 8, which was essentially a state constitutional amendment banning same-sex marriage. It was such a significant and divisive issue during the election that whether you were politically involved or not, and even if you didn't live in California, you probably remember it. Before the election and in the midst of a highly charged election season, I remember going to a gathering of pastors where they were trying to convince us that what we needed to do was rally our churches around that proposition.

They told us things like, if this doesn't pass, churches could lose their nonprofit status. If this doesn't pass, pastors could get thrown into prison. If this doesn't pass, our churches and our pastors could end up being sued. On and on and on they went through a list of things that were supposed to scare us enough to get our churches rallied around that proposition.

At our church in 2008, we didn't say a word about Proposition 8—and not because we were scared of offending people—which is what some people tried to say was true of us. We chose not to say anything about it because we refused and we continue to refuse to be driven by fear. We refuse to allow slippery-slope arguments, which are almost always fear-based arguments, to manipulate our church. Perfect love drives out fear.

Honestly, I don't understand why Christians in the church make so many decisions rooted in efforts to protect themselves. In the New Testament, the expectation is that Christians will suffer. The expectation is that the church will be persecuted. It's not that *some* Christians will suffer, that *some* churches will be persecuted. The expectation is that Christians will suffer, and the church will be persecuted.

It's not that we need to do things to try and suffer, and it's not that we need to do things intentionally to try to be persecuted, but I wonder why we spend so much time and energy —our resources, our finances—using politics to try and avoid suffering. The expectation in the New Testament is not that we would avoid suffering; it's that we would learn to suffer well.

In fact, I've realized things like whether or not churches get tax-exempt status is not my fight. It is entirely likely that during my lifetime churches will lose tax-exempt status, that there will be a time where you won't get a tax write-off for what you give to the church. I think it could end up being a good thing because it will force us to ask the question: Am I giving because the Lord calls me to give, or because I get a write-off at the end of the year.

Things like that are not my fight. I will not spend any energy fighting to try and make sure that churches maintain tax-exempt status. It is not my fight if the government tells us that we are not allowed to do certain things anymore. I will not fight that. None of that will change what we do, what we practice or what we believe as a church.

It doesn't matter what passes or what doesn't pass. As for my church, we will still continue to be the church God has called us to be. It doesn't matter what's legal or what's illegal. We will still continue to follow the teachings of the Scriptures. Nothing politically that happens will cause us to change what we do and what we believe.

Let's stop making decisions out of fear. Let's stop taking positions in an attempt to inoculate ourselves from anything happening to Christians or the church at large.

The reality is that the church thrives in persecution. Historically and even currently today, the places where the church is persecuted are the places where the church is growing the fastest. Historically it is when the church becomes too strongly linked and too strongly dependent on government that the church dies over time.

CHAPTER 4. The Spoils of Power

The church does not thrive where it's comfortable. In his book *Who Is This Man*, John Ortberg says, "Where the faith has too much money and too much power for too long it begins to spoil, and the center moves on." In the same book, Ortberg later says, "Jesus' followers have often behaved worse when they have possessed political power than when they were persecuted by it."[1]

We're being played, and we're letting it happen. Maybe we need to ask ourselves some questions about the stock we put in politics. Perhaps in the midst of all the politicking, bickering and pressure placed on any given election, maybe in the midst of it all we need to step back and ask: *As people of the kingdom, is this the way we're supposed to bring the kingdom into fruition?*

Some of you are very astute and at this point you're asking: *Doesn't the Bible have some instructions on how I'm supposed to relate to the government?* It does. The Bible gives just three basic instructions on how we are to relate to the government.

The first is to *follow the law*.

We follow the law. Romans 13:1-7 is about submitting to authorities and basically about following the law. It talks about basic responsibilities the government has, and they're essentially to create a structured and ordered society. Our responsibility is to submit to governmental laws as long as it doesn't contradict our following Christ.

We could spend a lot of time talking what it means to follow laws as long as they're not contradicting following Christ—and where that line is—but that's not the point of this book. So here's the important point from this passage: Our call is to follow the law.

The second calling we have around how we are to relate to the government is to *honor the emperor*.

1 Peter 2:17 talks about this. An emperor is a person who oversees the government, so in our system, the emperor is the president.

The question for us then is, how are you talking about presidential candidates? Men and women whom you may or may not agree with or care for are vying to be our emperor—these are men and women who could be our president—and Peter says to honor the emperor. When Peter wrote this, he was writing in a culture and at a time where there was not democracy as we know it today, so there weren't elected officials in the same way. They were not able to choose against a person in power. That wasn't their reality.

Our system of governance allows for us to vote against people who are in power. As a result of that, we have more opportunity to be able to express disagreement with people who are in power. But you can disagree with a person without degrading and demeaning the person. You can disagree with what they do and how they govern without vilifying them, without calling them names, without making accusations and without making assumptions.

What if in the midst of an election, we could just simply acknowledge that multiple people are running for this role and the way that we talk about them matters. The reality is, some of you reading this are not honoring them. You could choose to disagree with them in a way that honors them.

During the 2012 election, Carlos Whittaker[2], a Christian author and worship artist, blogged about starting a movement of people who did something they called "praying backwards." They gathered virtually to pray, and here's what they did: Mitt Romney supporters prayed for Barack Obama, and Obama supporters prayed for Romney. They prayed blessings over the person they were not voting for because that's a kingdom posture.

That's a posture that says the kingdom and its values are more important than my political party, and the kingdom and its values are more important than my political ideology. If you have a problem praying for the other team, praying honest blessings into their lives, maybe you need to ask yourself why that bothers you so much—because that's what people who have been formed by the kingdom do.

The third calling we have is to *pray for our leaders*.

1 Timothy 2:1-2 addresses praying for those in authority. It's important to remember that what is written in 1 Timothy, what is written in Romans, what is written in 1 Peter, all of this was incredibly subversive at the time it was

composed because the first-century government was largely anti-Christian. The goal for Christians of the time was not to try and change the government to get them to pass pro-Christian laws.

In the midst of talking about being persecuted for one's faith, and Peter extensively talks about being persecuted for one's faith, Peter says to honor the emperor. Do you realize the subversiveness of this? It wasn't, just get along and pledge allegiance to the flag. No, no—it was honor the emperor.

By the way, the emperor, Nero, was the one who ended up martyring Peter. Nero used Christians as scapegoats, and he started some of the most significant persecution of early Christians. Nero is the one who tied Christians to poles in his garden and lit them on fire. They would burn alive to light his garden parties. He was the one who would take Christians and have them killed by wild animals for sport. He would do it as a public spectacle.

Peter says to honor him. Essentially, it is a subversive way of saying the means matter. There is a way in which you live as a kingdom person, and even as you engage in systems that are completely different from Jesus and his kingdom, systems like government and politics —even as you do that, you are still to live as a kingdom person.

At my church, we made the commitment years ago to stay out of politics. We don't allow people to pass out petitions of any kind. We don't do voter registration drives. We don't distribute voter guides. We don't, as a church, march for or against political issues.

People have a problem with that. Every election some people try and push against that, saying, "Well, the church has to stand up for *these* things," whatever those things are for that person.

Here is my response to them: The church is called to stand up for one thing, and we'll stand up for that one thing. The church is called to stand up for Jesus. That is what we are called to stand up for.

CHAPTER 5. Christian Political Issues

I have a friend who is on the right side of the political spectrum. If you ever try to have a political conversation with this friend, every single issue comes back to abortion for him. Some of you might know somebody like this. Maybe some of you are this person. In fact, this friend once said: "Abortion is the singular most important Christian issue, and, when you vote, it trumps everything else you vote for."

He said that it's the single deciding factor when it comes to whether he'll vote for a candidate—regardless of the office for which the candidate is running. The candidate's other stances—and they have myriad other stances—and the candidate's lifestyle choices are all secondary to that. He believes passionately and wholeheartedly that this should be the most important issue for every Christian, and all other things are secondary to that.

When you talk to him about it, he cites verses that talk about God's care for human life, about how God knows you before you are born, and about Jesus' concern for children. This friend of mine on the right side of the political spectrum is a deeply committed Christian. He wants to live out what Jesus is calling him to. He believes that voting in this way is out of a deep Christian conviction.

I have this other friend who is on the left side of the political spectrum, and if you ever have a political conversation with her, what she continually brings up is God's care for the poor. She'll talk about how all throughout the Bible God has a heart and a bent toward those in poverty, about how he tends to align himself with the downtrodden and the mistreated.

For her, when she votes, she looks through a lens that filters candidates by whom she sees as having the greatest concern for the poor; which measures seem to evidence the greatest concern for the poor. She says there may be other positions candidates hold or stances they take that she disagrees with. There might even be lifestyle choices the candidates have that she disagrees with, but what's most significant for her is how a candidate is directly caring for the poor.

When you talk to her about it, she quotes all kinds of verses that back up her stance and her bent. This friend of mine is a deeply committed Christian. She wants to live out what Jesus is calling her to. She believes that voting in the way she does is out of her deep Christian convictions.

Here's the thing: These two friends of mine— both of whom are deeply committed Christians, both of whom want to live out the ways of Jesus —these two friends will vote for completely different candidates out of their Christian convictions.

Now, to be fair, my friend on the right would say it's not that he doesn't care for the poor, but that he believes there are other ways we should be caring for them in a different way than my friend on the left would say. My friend on the left cares very much about unborn children, but she believes the best way to care for them is at a systematic level by addressing poverty. Both of them, out of their deep Christian convictions, will vote in opposite directions.

So which one is right?

I mentioned earlier that during the 2008 presidential election I intentionally didn't make any political commentary from the stage at my church. That's not 100 percent accurate because I did say one thing. One weekend, before every service, I went out into our parking lot and counted bumper stickers on cars. I counted how many McCain/Palin bumper stickers there were and how many Obama/Biden bumper stickers there were. At every service, there was an almost equal amount of each bumper sticker.

So in each of the services on that weekend, I got up on stage and told people I had gone out to the parking lot and counted the bumper stickers, and I said, "I love that we have a church where both Obama supporters and McCain supporters can come together and worship together. I love that about our church." You would have thought by some people's reaction that I had lit the Bible on fire on stage and then danced on the apostle Paul's grave.

Obama supporters told me there was no way a Christian could vote for McCain and gave me their list of reasons why. McCain supporters said there was no way a Christian could vote for Obama and gave me their list of reasons why. What I saw as a reason to celebrate, other people saw as the church selling out, and which direction we were selling out was all dependent on their vantage point. It was all dependent on what causes they believed were the most Christian.

For committed Christians, this is what it seems to come down to, doesn't it? At first, it's about determining which issues you believe are Christian issues. And if you don't know which issues are Christian issues, there are plenty of people on the radio who will tell you, and there are plenty of people who will send you mailers to make sure you know which causes are Christian causes.

Then what you have to do is rank them in order of importance, because the reality is that for a democracy to work, it has to have compromise. So what you do is decide, well, *this* cause is more important than *these* causes, so I can compromise on *these* as long as I stay true to *this* one.

This is what my two friends have done. My one friend has said the most important Christian cause is caring for unborn children and seeing compromise on all of these other things because they're secondary. What my friend on the other side has said is that the most important Christian cause is caring for those in poverty and the downtrodden, so all this other stuff you can compromise on because *it's* secondary. So while they are both deeply committed Christians, if you were to put them in a room together, you would end up with fierce arguments about which is the most important Christian cause.

What, then, actually is the most important cause, or what is the most important issue? Do the Scriptures, as our authority, give any weight or any preference toward one cause over another? I believe they do. You'll be surprised to read this, I'm sure, but I believe we're having the wrong conversation. My two friends, who are both passionate about Jesus, both have it wrong. They are both having the wrong conversation.

CHAPTER 6. Jesus > Issues

The apostle Paul elevates one issue above everything else; one cause that he says is the most important. It's in Philippians 3:7. He says it in several places, but I think he's pretty poignant here:

> "But whatever were gains to me I now consider loss for the sake of Christ. What is more, I consider everything a loss because of the surpassing worth of knowing Christ Jesus my Lord, for whose sake I have lost all things. I consider them garbage, that I may gain Christ ..."

He says, there are all of these other things he could care about. There are all of these other things he could be passionate about. There are all of these other things he could devote his time to, his effort, his energy, and his resources to. They might all be good things, but he chooses to devote his time, energy, and passion in one direction and that one direction is to know Christ. It's to gain Christ.

He sets up this almost hyperbole showing a contrast between everything else and knowing Christ. Because of his pursuit of Christ, because he has decided that's the most important thing to pursue in his life, he says, everything else to me is garbage.

These lines of Paul in the New Testament were not originally written in English; they were written in Greek. Sometimes in translations, some of the nuance or some of the power of the original language can get lost.

The Greek word *skubalon* is often translated as garbage or as rubbish in this passage in Philippians. *Skubalon* is an incredibly intense word. The translations do not do it justice because it was essentially a first-century cuss word that meant dung or manure. It's best translation is a word we won't let our kids use.

Paul here is so intensely passionate about Jesus, so intensely passionate about a life that's focused on him, he says to him he considers everything else, compared to knowing Jesus, as *skubalon*. He's so passionate about Christ being first and foremost and being the most significant thing, the only way he can convey that is just to cuss in that moment. He says, compared to knowing Christ, it's *skubalon*.

For Paul and those first Christians, the cause they were deeply passionate about, the issue that rose above everything else, the thing they would be willing to give their lives for and say that everything else is secondary compared to, was Jesus. Simply Jesus. It wasn't causes associated with Jesus, and it wasn't issues you would assume Jesus cares about. It was simply Jesus. Everything else was *skubalon*.

Many people will say, well, yeah, Jesus should be our driving passion and our driving focus, but if he is, then we're going to care about *these* specific things, and *these* particular issues are going to be the things we should rally around. We should do that because of Jesus. That is not the way Paul or the early Christians saw it.

There are recorded instances where Paul stood before government officials and he could have talked about or said anything he wanted to. He could have called them to account for anything he wanted to call them to account for. He could have raised any concern or any issue and brought it to the forefront. Whatever it was he thought was an important issue or whatever he thought was an important issue to Jesus, he could have raised it there.

In Acts 25-26, there are recorded instances of Paul standing before government officials. He could talk about anything in front of them, and do you know what he chooses to talk about? Do you know what issue he raises? It's simply Jesus. It's Jesus having risen from the dead. Acts 26:28-29 reads:

> "Then Agrippa said to Paul, 'Do you think that in such a short time you can persuade me to be a Christian?' Paul replied, 'Short time or long—I pray to God that not only you but all who are listening to me today may become what I am, except for these chains.'"

Paul essentially says, here's my concern: It's that you would know Jesus.

There are all kinds of issues that were significant issues for first-century Christians, causes they cared about. When they have a chance to stand up before government officials, there is only one thing they bring up over and over and over again. It's Jesus—because to them, everything else is *skubalon*.

If they're going to offend the government, then it's going to be about Jesus, not because of issues. If they're going to get thrown in prison, it's going to be because of Jesus, not because of issues. If they're going to be mocked or ridiculed, it's going to be because of Jesus, not because of issues.

The book of Acts ends with that story of Paul under house arrest. When he's under house arrest, look at what his focus is and look which issues he raises. It's at the end of Acts 28. It says,

> "For two whole years Paul stayed there in his own rented house, " that's the house he was under house arrest in, "… and welcomed all who came to see him. He proclaimed the kingdom of God and taught about the Lord Jesus Christ—with all boldness and without hindrance!"

So, for what does he boldly stand? Jesus and his kingdom.

Paul could talk about the wrongful imprisonment of Christians because that's what he's facing. He has been wrongfully imprisoned and is in chains. He could talk about that. He could make that the thing to die for; he could fight to make sure Christians aren't wrongfully imprisoned. But he doesn't; it's not the issue. What he preaches boldly is simply Jesus and his kingdom. What he chooses to talk about is not issues that Christians care about during this time, and we know about issues they would have cared about at this time. He focuses instead on the person of Jesus. For the early church, there was no cause but Christ.

What we often do with issues is say, *well, Christians should care about this particular thing.* By the way, there are issues on the right side of the political spectrum that Christians should care about, and there are issues on the left side of the political spectrum that Christians should care about. Which ones are more important to you are usually defined by your political ideology, not by your theology.

When deciding which is more important—Jesus or issues—we often end up mixing the two. What Paul does when he stands up before government officials is he lifts up the person of Jesus, not the issues he could associate with Jesus. The reality is sometimes in our focus on issues we push people away from Jesus.

We have to decide what is more important to us. Is making our view on an issue know the most important thing, or is making Jesus known more important than the issue at hand? If we have one thing we can share, it should be Jesus. If you're going to offend someone, let them be offended by the person of Jesus Christ. Jesus is so much more important than your political priorities or parties.

Following Christ demands that your allegiance is to him and not to your political party or your political issues. In fact, if your allegiance is to Christ and you belong to a political party, then there should be things that are a part of your political party that should bother you. For instance, Republicans, you should be incredibly concerned with the way that Republicans talk about immigrants. When language is used that does not reflect the significance of how every person is created in the image of God, then you should have an issue.

Democrats, you should be incredibly concerned with the way that Democrats value individual choice over unborn human life. It should bother you that there is a dismissal of the inherent value of each and every life. God gives each life value, and no one has the right to take that away.

The more time you spend defending your party's views and issues, the more likely it is that you're missing the prophetic nature of what it means to follow Jesus. Following Jesus means your allegiance is to him. It means being able to stand outside of something, not becoming so enmeshed in it that you're unable to call out of it the things that are not in alignment with your primary allegiance.

Our political views can become the vantage point through which we view the Scriptures and our faith, and the more invested we become in a political viewpoint, the more our faith can become skewed by that viewpoint. But the opposite is true as well—your faith can have an effect on your politics, and not always in the way that you would expect.

In 2007, Baylor University published a study that showed that the frequency of Bible reading has an effect on your politics.[1] The study found that the more frequently you read the Bible, the less likely you are to fall in line with the views of any particular political party. What's fascinating to me is that the more frequently you read the Bible, the more likely you are to have some views that are considered more conservative politically, but you are also more liable to have some views that are considered more liberal politically.

It found that frequent Bible reading makes you more likely to be opposed to abortion, which is typically considered a more conservative view politically. It also found, however, that if you read the Bible frequently that you're 45% more likely to support abolishing the death penalty, which is typically a more liberal viewpoint. In other words, when we engage the Scriptures and allow them to be formative in our worldview, we end up in a place that neither party adequately represents.

What can happen, however, is that we get so passionate about our political party and political issues that we end up putting them in the wrong place in our lives. We have often confused Jesus with issues and they are not the same thing. In fact, we often end up making an idol of our issues.

Tim Keller, in his book *Counterfeit Gods*, defines an idol as "anything more important to you than God, anything that absorbs your heart and your imagination more than God, anything you seek to give you what only God can give." An idol is "anything so central and essential to your life that, should you lose it, your life would feel hardly worth living." He says "Idols are good things turned into ultimate things."

This is what we do: We take good things, and we make them the center of our lives.[2]

Some of us do this with our family. Family is an incredibly good thing, but when it begins to consume you—and you make it the center of your life and everything revolves around your family—you make your family your idol.

It could be your job—this good thing in your life that enables you to provide for yourself and your family that at some point starts to drive you, becoming the center of your life. Just as easily, it could be your political ideology. It could be your political party that you're making an idol, or it could be other good and significant issues that you care about.

Caring for the unborn is a good issue that can become an idol. Caring for those in poverty and the downtrodden are good issues that can become idols. Idols in our lives are rarely bad things. They're usually good things that slowly starts taking on more and more importance. It's a different thing to make Jesus the center of your life than it is to make issues you believe Jesus cares about the center of your life. Those are two different things.

What do you think people who know you would say drives you during election season? Is what drives you during election season getting people to vote yes on a certain proposition? Is it getting a candidate back into the White House, or is it getting a person or party out of the White House? Whatever it is that consumes you, you have likely made it an idol.

It's usually not a bad thing you make into an idol. It could be a very good thing or a very good cause, but as soon as it starts driving you, as soon as it starts consuming you, you have made it an idol. If it's not *skubalon* to you compared to Jesus, it is likely an idol.

I referenced Proposition 8 in an earlier chapter. I remember people who were passionate about Prop 8 during the election and had signs in their yards, and I remember talking to a couple of those people. I asked them, "If that sign in your yard was pushing people away from Jesus, would you be willing to take it down?" Every single person I asked said, "No." They attempted to explain their reasoning, adding, "No, because I am standing up for truth by putting this in my yard." That's an idol.

Paul wasn't trying to offend people outside of the church with issues. He said, *if they're going to be offended, let it be with the cross of Christ.* Too many of us have confused Jesus with issues. We've said, *well, it's okay to offend people as long as it's a right issue.* I think the apostle Paul would say to that, *No, no, no. It is okay to offend people with the person of Jesus, but not with the issues.*

CHAPTER 7. Morality and Following Jesus

The goal of the church is not to export morality to the rest of society. Our goal as a church is to help the rest of society to encounter the resurrected Jesus. For instance, when you read lists of sins in the New Testament, they aren't there for you to go and impose on other people outside of the church. They are there to speak conviction *to* the church.

Every time you find a list of sins, it is written to a specific audience—a church—to convict that church because the people of the church have surrendered their lives and submitted themselves to Jesus. As a result of that, they've chosen to live their lives oriented in a certain direction. We have chosen, as people of the kingdom, as people who follow Jesus, to submit to kingdom ethics and kingdom morality because we have submitted our lives to Christ.

Sometimes we're trying to force everyone else to submit to those same ethics and that same morality without a submission to Jesus. Paul says it this way in 1 Corinthians 5:

> "What business is it of mine to judge those outside the church?"

Sometimes what happens in our effort to lift up issues is we end up holding people who are outside of Christ to the standards of Christ without their submitting to Christ.

The church is not called to be the moral police for the rest of society. The church is called to call its own people to a kingdom morality, and it's called to draw those who are outside of the church to Jesus. Far too often, in the way we engage in politics, it's about trying to treat the rest of society like they are the church.

As I've discussed these ideas with people, I've heard myriad responses. People have said things such as, *you know what your problem is, you're just afraid of being offensive.* If you know me, you know that's not it at all. It's not that I'm afraid of offending people, it's that if I'm going to offend people, then I want to offend them with the right things.

Calling people on sin and calling people to certain standards of living is for the church, and it's for the church to be offended by that. The call of the New Testament is not to offend those outside the church with those standards. Here's what should be offensive to those outside the church. It should be the person of Jesus: his death, his burial, his resurrection. It's Jesus and the radical, scandalized grace that he offers. We have confused Jesus with issues.

Remember who Jesus had the most conflict with —it was the Pharisees, the religious leaders of his day. This group is whom he offended the most, because he was speaking to people who had already subscribed to a certain moral ethic and moral code.

But do you know who was most attracted to Jesus? Tax collectors and prostitutes—the people in the day who were considered sinners, who were considered the farthest outside of God's community, the people who were living the least like God wanted them to. What we have to do is look at our churches today and the people who are most attracted to us, and we have to ask, *are they the same as those who were most attracted to Jesus?* The answer, unfortunately, is usually no.

If that's the case, then we have to ask ourselves, *well, then why is it that the church doesn't attract the same kinds of people Jesus attracted*? Could one of the reasons be that Jesus didn't have political platforms against any of them? It's incredibly hard for a person to be attracted to the church when the church actively rallies and lobbies against them. As a kingdom people, the kingdom question is not, *how should we vote*, but instead it's, *how should we live*. Voting doesn't cost us much, but a kingdom lifestyle does.

CHAPTER 8. The Early Church Model

One model worth considering is the early church and the way in which it dealt with societal moral issues during its time.

In the early church, one of the more significant causes for them was infanticide. John Ortberg talks about it this way in *Who Is This Man*?:

> "In the ancient world, unwanted children were often simply left to die, a practice called 'exposure'. The head of the household had the legal right decide the life or death of other members of the family. This decision was usually made during the first eight days or so of life. (Plutarch wrote that until that time the child was 'more like a plant than a human being.')"

Ortberg goes on to say, "The most common reasons to expose a child would be if a family lived in poverty, or if a wealthy family did not want the estate divided up, or if the child was the wrong gender (meaning a girl ...), or if the child were illegitimate."

The conditions under which children were "exposed" are horrifying. The practice was carried out in a variety of ways. "Abandoned children were often left on a dump or a dung hill. They most often died; sometimes they were rescued, but usually this was to become enslaved."

Slave children were given insulting names that were the equivalent of calling them dung so that people would know where they came from—and so that for the remainder of their lives they would be marked and scarred.[1]

Twenty-five percent of all children born during this time didn't make it to their first birthday, and infanticide was a common and accepted practice throughout the Roman Empire, which contributes to that statistic. Children were seen as disposable in the first century.

To the first followers of Jesus, to those first Christians, you can imagine this practice was unacceptable. They followed a Jesus who valued children. They followed a Jesus who said that each person was created in the very image of God. You find writings from the early church going back to the second century, where within the church they're prohibiting the widespread practice of abortion and infanticide at that time.[2]

But here's what you do not find: You don't find a lot of politicking about it. In fact, it's hard to find much, if even any, politicking about it. You don't find people standing before the emperor arguing about this vile practice. When they stand before the emperor, they follow Paul's example, and they lift up Jesus and his resurrection.

Even though they believed this was an issue that Jesus cared about, even though they taught on it in their churches, they did not confuse lifting up Jesus with lifting up an issue. Here's what they did instead: They began to live in a way that inconvenienced their own lives to care about what they valued. They didn't politick on it. They didn't write letters to the government. They didn't do whatever the ancient equivalent of blogging was to deal with it. Instead, they lived it.

What those early Christians began to do was teach in their churches the value of children. Ortberg mentions that you had some, like Saint Ambrose of Milan, who began to talk about not only caring for children, but actually about caring for the poor, because they recognized that poverty often destroyed people's capacity to care for children, and it would lead to practices like exposure.

Those early Christians were taken with the kingdom vision of Jesus, and as they became more and more swept up in this kingdom vision, they began to live it out. Christians would go to the dump, and as children were placed at the dump, they would intervene before slave traders would get there and rescue the children who were there, bringing them into their own homes, inconveniencing themselves to raise those children as their own.[3]

In fact, some believe that James, when he writes that pure religion is to look after the orphans, is directly referring to this practice. Recognizing the financial strain this would create for some families, and even understanding the link between poverty and exposure of children, the church began to collect money and distribute it to those who had needs.

This beautiful community emerges, where people are intentionally going after abandoned children, inconveniencing themselves to bring them into their homes. Where those who have resources are giving them up to help those who don't; where those who have resources are sacrificing to help others under greater financial strain because they're raising these children.

None of these efforts were focused on changing laws. None of these efforts were focused on changing the government's attitude toward infanticide and exposure, even though it was outrageous to Christians that it was happening. Their focus was not on changing laws and changing the government; it was on living out the kingdom kind of life that Jesus had called them to, which is so much harder to do.

What's interesting is what began to happen. Pretty soon, orphanages began to emerge, as there were more and more children who needed to be cared for. Parents began bringing their children not to the dumps, but to the doorsteps of monasteries and churches and orphanages because the Christians became known as the people who would care for these unwanted children.[4]

"By the late fourth century, a Christian emperor outlawed the practice of exposure for the entire empire,"[5] not because he ran on the platform of getting rid of it, and not because Christians rallied together to get a ballot measure passed.

Because of Christians living this out, inconveniencing themselves, dying to themselves to live out this kingdom vision, it slowly began to infiltrate society.[6] Maybe it's like yeast working its way through dough.

Over time, the collective societal consciousness toward children began to change. It started to change in such a way where society now would look at a practice like that and say, that is ridiculous and terrible, and that should not happen. It changed because the collective consciousness slowly over time began to change.

A law eventually was enacted—not because of lobbyists, and not because of picketing, and not because some pastors rallied the troops to put pressure on the government—but because slowly, over time, an entire community's posture toward children changed because of the sacrificial nature with which the Christians lived out their faith.

That's how the kingdom grows. It grows through service, sacrifice, and death. And it happens slowly. It took hundreds of years before laws were passed. It wasn't some quick thing because that wasn't their goal. Their goal was not to change laws; it was to live it out. As a result, laws ended up changing, but it was never their goal.

There's a subtle but significant difference between the two. Laws can end up getting changed, but that is not our goal, and that is not our rallying cry. Jesus is our rallying cry, and our goal is to live out his kingdom ways. As we do that, along the way some laws and government postures will change as an indirect result—but many won't, and that's not our goal.

When those first Christians were in front of the emperor, in front of kings, in front of government officials, they lifted up Jesus, not issues, and they inconvenienced themselves because of the issues Jesus would care about.

The first Christians were actually incredibly political in a way, but not in the way we would think of them being political or politically involved. It was in a much, much more subversive way. The first Christians co-opted political language and began applying it to Jesus because they wanted to convey the significance of Jesus and the importance of their allegiance toward him.[6]

Titles that were reserved for Caesar, the emperor, were then taken from Caesar by the Christians and began to get applied to Jesus; titles like Lord. When we declare Jesus as Lord, that is those first Christians taking a title that was reserved for Caesar and saying, I'm going to call Jesus Lord. In fact, there are a few political propaganda lines that were used for Caesar that the first Christians began to take and co-opt and use for Jesus.[7]

Here's one of them they used. There was a phrase used which we have printed on coins from the first century and before that. It said, "There is no name under heaven by which men can be saved except for that of Caesar." Maybe some of you remember in Acts 4 that what the early Christians say is,

> "There is no name under heaven by which men can be saved except for that of Jesus."

They didn't make that line up. They took political propaganda of the day, and they took Caesar's name out and put Jesus' name in.[8] They took the common political language of the day and co-opted it for Jesus. I mean, do you realize how incredibly subversive this is? They were essentially saying, Jesus is our ruler. He is the one we follow. He is above, and he is greater than whoever is here ruling us because everything else is *skubalon.*

Several people have suggested that the best way to understand the phrase "Jesus is Lord" today is to say "Jesus is president," because it wasn't just about saying I follow Jesus. It was also about saying I follow Jesus *instead of.* I follow Jesus, and he replaces *this.* So you find phrases in the New Testament like this: Paul says in Philippians 3,

> "Our citizenship is in heaven."

To seek Jesus above everything else began to have numerous implications for them.

I think of what Jesus says in Luke 14. He says,

> "If anyone comes to me and does not hate father and mother, wife and children, brothers and sisters—yes, even their own life—such a person cannot be my disciple."

Let that sink in for a minute. It can be easy, once you've been around the Scriptures for a while, to get used to statements like that—statements that actually should evoke a strong reaction. Let the weight of what Jesus says sink in.

> "If anyone comes to me and does not hate his father and mother, wife and children, brothers and sisters, even his own life, he can't be my disciple."

It's this call to follow him and to say, everything else is *skubalon*.

Here's what I understand Jesus to be saying: If you follow him, it will require such an abandonment of everything else, such a passionate pursuit of him and his kingdom, that it will appear to others as though you hate the very relationships that should be closest to you. Because of your abandonment of everything else and because of your pursuit of Jesus, that's what it will look like to those who don't have that same passionate pursuit.

I don't think Jesus is literally telling people to hate their parents and wives and children because at other times he says the opposite of that. He says to honor your parents. So he's not saying, try and hate those closest to you—but he is saying, pursue me with such passion and such abandonment that that is what it's going to end up looking like.

Now if that is true of relationships that are closest to us, wouldn't it stand to reason that would also be true of relationships that get farther and farther away? Couldn't you substitute neighbors in there, or couldn't you substitute job in there? Jesus is saying, if anyone doesn't come after me and hate his own job, he can't be my disciple. Some of you have no problem with that idea.

But couldn't we keep going with that and say our political party? *If any Republicans don't come to me and hate Republicans, if any Democrats don't come after me and hate Democrats ...* That would make sense because if it's going to be true of those who are closest to us, it would also be true of relationships that are less close to us. Couldn't you keep going with that, then? Couldn't you say that would even be true of your country? *If anyone comes to me and does not hate his own country, he cannot be my disciple.*

Here's what's interesting to me: When I've said that to people, and even when I've made statements like that in sermons, most people have had a visceral reaction to hearing it. Maybe you even did just reading that.

I find this incredibly interesting because most Christians are perfectly fine with Jesus saying, "Hate your father and mother." We're perfectly fine with Jesus saying, "Hate your wife and your children, your brothers and your sisters." We're perfectly fine with Jesus saying, "Hate even your own life—" but we then have a visceral reaction if we insert country in there.

If that stings you in some way, maybe you need to ask why. Why are we okay with Jesus saying to hate those closest to us, but if we substitute those closest with our country, it doesn't sit well? Could it be that some of us have made our country an idol? Jesus is not only greater than issues, but he is also greater than your country, whichever country that is.

It seems that in any given election in the United States, what's expected of a candidate is that they put an inordinate amount of emphasis on the extraordinariness of America. In 2012, Governor Mitt Romney said that America is the hope of the earth, and President Barack Obama said that America is the only indispensable nation. Let me just ask this: Is that a kingdom-first posture, or is that a country-first posture?

A kingdom-first posture says that Jesus is the only hope of the earth. A kingdom-first posture says the kingdom is the only thing that's indispensable. Before I get misquoted all over the Internet, I don't think Jesus is saying to hate your own country, but I do think he's saying that if you pursue him with the abandonment and the passion he calls for, it will appear to those who do not pursue him in that same way like you hate those things closest to you, because everything else is *skubalon*.

CONCLUSION. Unity in Christ

In the second century, a man named Mathetes, who was not a Christian, wrote a letter to a man named Diognetus, who also was not a Christian. Both men were writing to each other, trying to make sense of Christians. Mathetes' letter is called the Epistle of Mathetes. Here's basically what he says.

> "Christians are not distinguished from the rest of mankind, either in locality [they live where everyone else lives], or in speech [they talk the same way we do], or in customs [they kind of do the same things we do; they have the same practices] ... But while they dwell in cities of Greeks and barbarians as the lot of each is cast [they end up in all of these different places] ... the constitution of their own citizenship is marvelous and confessedly contradicts expectation. They dwell in their own countries, but only as sojourners [only as those who are just sort of passing through]. Every foreign country is a fatherland to them, and every fatherland is a foreign."

The Christians were first and foremost bound by their identity in Christ before geopolitical boundaries bound them. They were first and foremost bound together as brothers and sisters in Christ with a citizenship that transcended national man-made borders. The kingdom of God does not have national boundaries.

There is no such thing in the New Testament as a Christian nation. It doesn't matter to me whether the forefathers intended it to be or not. That's not the discussion to me. The discussion to me, because the Bible is my authority, is, does the New Testament know a Christian nation? It does not. The only Christian nation the New Testament knows is the kingdom of God, which transcends geographical boundaries. It transcends them all.

So what the kingdom does is, when you first seek Jesus, it takes all of the boundaries we tend to put up and it begins tearing them down. It says we are united in Christ before these things that divide us, because to us, first and foremost, everything else is *skubalon*. We are first united in Christ before we are Americans, and we are first united in Christ before we're Democrats or Republicans. We are first united in Christ before we are free market or communist or socialist.

We are first united in Christ.

Far too often, politics infiltrates the church and the church becomes divided. We become divided from our brothers and our sisters who live in other countries or who have a different political ideology. That kind of thing is not a new problem. The apostle Paul had to deal with significant divisions in the early church in the first century. In a letter to the church in Corinth he writes,

> "In the first place, I hear that when you come together as a church, there are divisions among you, and to some extent I believe it."
> (1 Corinthians 11:18)

The divisions he's talking about are socioeconomic divisions. The poor and the rich begin to create a divide in the church. Those who are rich are kind of trampling over those who are poor, and there begins to become this division in the church in Corinth. They have the rich, and they have the poor, who are not united in Christ. They're united around socioeconomics.

He goes on, talking about the practice of Communion or the Lord's Supper,

> "So then, whoever eats the bread or drinks the cup of the Lord in an unworthy manner will be guilty of sinning against the body [the church] and blood of the Lord. Everyone ought to examine themselves before they eat of the bread and drink from the cup. For those who eat and drink without discerning the body of Christ eat and drink judgment on themselves"
> (1 Corinthians 11:27-28)

What's happening during Paul's time is the rich are going first to take communion, and they're taking it all, and there's nothing left over for the poor. Paul let's them know it is unacceptable to eat the bread and drink the cup with divisions in the body, because we are first united as brothers and sisters in Christ before we are divided over man-made issues.

When he writes here with stern language about eating and drinking the cup in an unworthy manner, when he talks about eating and drinking in a way that brings judgment on yourself, he is not talking about personal sin.

What he is talking about is divisions within the body. He says, "What you are doing is eating and drinking judgment on yourself if you are taking the Lord's Supper, all the while maintaining divisions within the body."

If you are creating divisions within the body of Christ, you are eating and drinking the cup in an unworthy manner. If you have animosity toward your brothers and sisters in Christ who are Democrats; if you have animosity toward your brothers and sisters in Christ who are Republicans; if you have animosity toward your brothers and sisters in Christ who are Libertarians or Tea Party members or socialists; or with people who are just indifferent to the whole thing and just don't care about the political process—then you are eating the bread and drinking the cup in an unworthy manner.

Before I'm an American, before I'm a Democrat, before I'm a Republican, before I'm a socialist, before I'm a Tea Party member, before I'm indifferent—before any of those things—I am first and foremost a citizen of the kingdom of God. I will be united with my brothers and sisters in Christ before any of those things.

The beauty of the church is that we are first united in Christ before we are divided over anything else. The bread and the cup are these incredibly subversive emblems that say, we are united with Christ and with our brothers and sisters in Christ before anything else. That is first and foremost, and everything else is *skubalon*.

APPENDIX

A PRAYER

I want to conclude this book by offering a prayer. My hope is that this prayer might be useful to you during each political season. In moments when you find yourself getting overly focused on politics, may this prayer be something that you use to re-center yourself. When you are frustrated because you've had a heated political conversation with a friend, or because an election doesn't seem to be going your way, perhaps this prayer will be useful. It could be that you are still trying to figure out what the role of your faith is as it relates to politics, and as you engage in that journey, may this prayer be one that helps guide you.

"God,

Help me to be someone who pursues what you desire, in the way that you want me to pursue it. Open up my mind and my heart to what that looks like.

I choose to put my hope in you. I recognize that all systems of government will fall short, and so I choose to seek first, not the kingdom of my country, but instead the kingdom of God. Help me to be driven by love and never by fear.

May I be someone who first and foremost seeks to point people to Jesus. Please reveal to me, and convict me of, areas in my life where my commitment and zeal for political issues has hindered me from doing that.

For our leaders whom I agree with, bless them.
For our leaders whom I disagree with, bless them.

May their lives and their families experience the blessings of a life under your care.

For those leaders whom I have been disrespectful towards, forgive me.
For those leaders whom I have a hard heart towards, soften my heart.

In places where I have allowed my political views to cause walls between my brothers and sisters in Christ, would you tear down those walls? Show me where I need to seek reconciliation as a result of my behavior, and teach me how to live in unity with my fellow believers.

Jesus, may your kingdom come, your will be done, on earth as it is in heaven.

Amen."

ABOUT THE AUTHOR

Mike Goldsworthy serves as the lead pastor at Parkcrest Christian Church in Long Beach, California. In addition to serving at his church, Mike is the co-founder of PlantLB, a multi-ethnic, multi-denominational, city-centric church planting effort in the greater Long Beach area. He and his wife, Allison, have been married for 15 years and have two kids, Isaac, and Kate. They can regularly be found hiking, camping, biking, and playing board games together.

He can be found online at mikegoldsworthy.com

BIBLIOGRAPHY

A Nation of Drunkards: Prohibition--A Film by Ken Burns and Lynn Novick. PBS, 2011.

A Nation of Scofflaws: Prohibition--A Film by Ken Burns and Lynn Novick. PBS, 2011.

A Nation of Scofflaws: Prohibition--A Film by Ken Burns and Lynn Novick. PBS, 2011.

Bartholomew, Craig G. *A Royal Priesthood?: The Use of the Bible Ethically and Politically.* Grand Rapids, MI: Zondervan, 2002.

Blocker, Jack S., David M. Fahey, and Ian R. Tyrrell. *Alcohol and Temperance in Modern History: An International Encyclopedia.* Santa Barbara, CA: ABC-CLIO, 2003.

Boyd, Gregory A. *The Myth of a Christian Nation: How the Quest for Political Power Is Destroying the Church.* Grand Rapids, MI: Zondervan, 2005.

Engdahl, Sylvia. *Amendments XVIII and XXI: Prohibition and Repeal.* Farmington Hills, MI: Greenhaven Press, 2009.

Fox, Robin Lane. *Pagans and Christians.* New York: Knopf, 1987.

Franzen, Aaron B. "Survey: Frequent Bible Reading Can Turn You Liberal." ChristianityToday.com. October 12, 2011. Accessed January 30, 2016. http://www.christianitytoday.com/ct/2011/october/survey-bible-reading-liberal.html.

González, Justo L. *The Story of Christianity*. San Francisco: Harper & Row, 1984.

Keller, Timothy. *Counterfeit Gods: The Empty Promises of Money, Sex, and Power, and the Only Hope That Matters*. New York: Dutton, 2009.

Lewis, Ted. *Electing Not to Vote: Christian Reflections on Reasons for Not Voting*. Eugene, OR: Cascade Books, 2008.

McCullough, David G. *John Adams*. New York: Simon & Schuster, 2001.

Ortberg, John. *Who Is This Man?: The Unpredictable Impact of the Inescapable Jesus*. Grand Rapids, MI: Zondervan, 2012.

Scherer, Michael. "Blue Truth, Red Truth." *Time*, October 03, 2012.

Thomas, Cal, and Ed Dobson. *Blinded by Might: Can the Religious Right Save America?* Grand Rapids, MI: Zondervan Pub. House, 1999.

NOTES

Introduction
1. Scherer, "Blue Truth, Red Truth."

Chapter. 2
1. Thomas and Dobson, *Blinded by Might.*
2. Boyd, *The Myth of a Christian Nation,* 18.
3. Gonzaĺez, *The Story of Christianity,* 374-375.
4, 5, 6. Burns and Novick, "Prohibition."
7. Blocker, Fahey, Tyrrell, *Alcohol and Temperance in Modern History.*
8. Engdahl, *Amendments XVIII and XXI: Prohibition and Repeal.*
9. http://www.celebraterecovery.com.
10. Lewis, *Electing Not to Vote.*

Chapter 3
1. McCullough, *John Addams*
2. Scherer, "Blue Truth, Red Truth."

Chapter 4
1. Ortberg, *Who Is This Man?.*
2. http://www.carloswhittaker.com

Chapter 6
1. Franzen, "Survey: Frequent Bible Reading Can Turn You Liberal."

Chapter 8
1. Ortberg, *Who Is This Man?.*
2. See The Didache, or *"The Teaching of the Twelve Apostles."*
3, 4, 5. Ortberg, *Who Is This Man?*

6.   Fox, *Pagans and Christians*.
7, 8. Bartholomew, *A Royal Priesthood?*.

55468716R00070

Made in the USA
Charleston, SC
29 April 2016